THE KEY

THE KEY

Unlock Your Psychic Abilities

A Self-Guided Course with CD

ECHO BODINE

New World Library
Novato, California

New World Library
14 Pamaron Way
Novato, California 94949

Text design and typography by Mary Ann Casler
Developed by Vanessa Brown
Edited by Heather Hutson Moro
Copyedited by Kristen Cashman and Ellen Winkler

Library of Congress Cataloging-in-Publication Data
Bodine, Echo L.
The key : unlock your psychic abilities / Echo Bodine.
    p.   cm.
ISBN-13: 978-1-57731-549-0 (hardcover with audio cd : alk. paper)
1. Psychic ability. I. Title.
BF1031.B613 2003
133.8—dc22   2006010034

First printing, October 2006
ISBN-10: 1-57731-549-9
ISBN-13: 978-1-57731-549-0
Printed in Hong Kong

Distributed by Publishers Group West

10 9 8 7 6 5 4 3 2 1

CONTENTS

CHAPTER 3:
UNDERSTANDING PSYCHIC INFORMATION   37

CHAPTER 4:

BASIC PSYCHIC DEVELOPMENT EXERCISES   67

CHAPTER 5:

PROGRESS JOURNAL   115

INTRODUCTION

Each of us has psychic abilities to some degree. But they're usually very subtle, so most of the time when we use them, we don't realize that's what we're doing.

Has a picture ever popped into your head that revealed the answer to something you'd been wondering about? Has a thought ever occurred to you out of nowhere that was the guidance you were praying for? Have you ever sensed something about a person that wasn't based on anything you consciously knew, but it later turned out to be true? Every day at least one of your psychic abilities helps you in some way.

As a psychic, healer, and teacher, I've been using these abilities for close to forty years. But you don't have to become a professional to develop your psychic abilities. Pictures, thoughts, and feelings come to you psychically from God and your guides. These are primarily meant to help you with whatever life experience you happen to be dealing with. So, developing your psychic gifts is a way to improve the way you live your life; it's not necessarily the start of a career.

When God created us, He gave us unlimited potential. Our soul's goal is to discover and develop this potential in all areas of our lives. We couldn't possibly finish the job in one lifetime, which is one of the reasons why we continue to reincarnate here on Earth. If you're feeling called to explore your psychic gifts, your soul has either chosen to begin your metaphysical development in this lifetime or to continue this development from previous lives. So let's get down to business!

HOW TO USE THE KEY

This book and CD set is a step-by-step psychic development course to help you tap into and refine your psychic abilities. In these pages, I describe the different types of psychic abilities and how they work. In addition, I provide strategies for staying grounded, developing boundaries, and avoiding common pitfalls you may encounter as you practice. I also give you simple exercises to help you develop your abilities.

Throughout this book you'll find journaling prompts, as well as pages on which to record your thoughts as you progress, including a dedicated journal section at the end. Try to write something about your spiritual path or psychic development every day. Later, you'll enjoy looking back at these entries to see how much you've grown psychically. On the CD, I provide guided meditations and visualizations that correspond to key steps in your psychic development journey.

If you would like to learn more about psychics and psychic abilities, including what the Bible has to say about them, I encourage you to also read my book *The Gift*, in which these topics are explored more thoroughly.

TO ALL PSYCHICS IN TRAINING

If you're in your first year of development and you start doing mini-readings for people, be sure to tell them you're still in training. Once in a while, a newly graduated student will get some business cards made up at the end of my thirteen-week class, thinking she or he is ready to start doing readings for a living. There is so much to learn about interpreting and understanding these gifts that there is no way a person could be ready that quickly. I practiced on friends and family members for twelve years before doing this work full-time. This doesn't mean it's going to take you that long, but it will take time.

If you're in a crummy job and are hoping to develop your abilities so you can set up shop as a psychic instead, I suggest you find a different job while you're taking the time to cultivate your gifts. You don't need the added pressure of having to develop your gifts quickly; that pressure would just interfere with your development.

A SPECIAL NOTE TO TEENAGERS

If you are a teenager hoping to develop your psychic abilities now, please consider waiting a few years, until you get more experience and wisdom under your belt. Put the whole issue on hold. Teenagers go through enough changes as it is, and opening up psychically could be too much. There is a tremendous responsibility that goes along with being psychic, and many teenagers aren't emotionally mature enough to handle it yet.

Once you've become an independent adult, you can return to all of this and explore whether or not you want to do anything with your psychic gifts. I promise you, they won't go away. Don't make your life more complicated than it already is or burden yourself with any added responsibility.

A SPECIAL NOTE TO CHRISTIAN READERS

Throughout my life as a psychic, I've had more than my share of fundamentalist Christians tell me that according to the Bible the work I do is evil, that I work for Satan, and that I'm going straight to hell. Actually, I am a Christian myself, and I once struggled with the question of whether my abilities and my faith were incompatible. I've seen many of my students engaged in the same struggle.

I want to reassure Christian readers that they aren't rejecting their religion by developing their psychic abilities.

The Bible itself does not support the idea that psychic abilities are evil. I have gone through the scriptures of both the Old and New Testaments with a fine-tooth comb searching for any reference to prophets, seers, fortune-tellers, diviners, enchanters, and so on. I've read books about the Bible and watched documentaries about biblical times. I may not be a biblical scholar, but I wanted to do a thorough job and to understand, as much as we can know today, what the Bible actually says about psychic abilities. In my book *The Gift*, a whole chapter is devoted to what I found, but here is a quick idea.

By my count, the Old Testament contains close to five hundred references to seers and prophets (those two terms were synonymous in biblical times), and the majority of them are positive. One thing the Old Testament makes very clear is that prophets and fortune-tellers are *not* the same thing. Prophets were considered to be messengers of God, whereas fortune-tellers were clumped in the same category as sorcerers, diviners, and enchanters. (See Leviticus 19:26, Leviticus 19:31, Leviticus 20:6, and Deuteronomy 18:10–14.)

These scriptures make perfect sense to me, and none of them say that what I do for people is wrong. They *do* say not to turn to fortune-tellers but to turn to God; not to get distracted by sorcerers or enchanters; and not to get involved in black magic and hurt others.

The New Testament mainly describes the ministry and death of Jesus, who was a Hebrew rabbi named Jeshua Ben Joseph, which translates as "Teacher Jesus son of Joseph." After Jesus's crucifixion, the New Testament describes the acts of his disciples (or apostles) and the beginnings of Christianity. Before his crucifixion, Jesus told his disciples that God was going to send another comforter (or counselor) who would never leave us, and that counselor is the Holy Spirit (John 14:16).

According to the Bible, after the death of Jesus, Paul became one of the men spreading Jesus's teachings. In Paul's letters to the Corinthians, he talks about the "Gifts of the Spirit." This is where we clearly see that the counselor that Jesus referred to (the Holy Spirit) has given all of us the "Gift of Prophecy" (1 Corinthians 12). 1 Corinthians 12:8–11 says:

And now, dear brothers and sisters, I will write about the special abilities the Holy Spirit gives to each of us, for I must correct your misunder standings about them. To one person the Spirit gives the ability to give wise advice; to another he gives the gift of special knowledge. He gives special faith to another and to someone else the power to heal the sick. He gives one person the power to perform miracles, and to another the ability to prophesy. He gives someone else the ability to know whether it is really the Spirit of God or another spirit that is speaking. Still another person is given the ability to speak in unknown languages, and another is given the ability to interpret what is being said. It is the one and only Holy Spirit who distributes these gifts. He alone decides which gift each person should have.

It should be noted that nowhere in Corinthians are the words *evil* or *Satan* ever mentioned when Paul is describing the Gifts of the Spirit, and he clearly points out that the Gift of Prophecy (which is the result of psychic abilities) comes from the Holy Spirit.

I hold out hope that someday our religious leaders will stop disparaging psychic abilities and acknowledge them as special gifts from the Holy Spirit. I have no idea how long this is going to take. But I believe if we just keep moving forward, asking God to guide us with our Gifts of the Spirit, we'll know what to do. We can't let the prejudices and negative opinions of others slow us down.

I am so grateful I didn't cave in years ago when certain friends of mine asked me to give up my gifts. I'm so grateful I've continued to live by the voice within rather than the negative, fearful voices outside me. In the end, it all boils down to a simple question: Are we acting on faith or fear? Are we listening to God or the world?

Describe your feelings about or experience with psychic phenomena. Have you ever felt your psychic abilities were helping you in some way?

CHAPTER 1

PSYCHIC BASICS

To start, let's take a look at what types
of psychic gifts people can have and how they all
work to provide us with information.

THE FOUR PSYCHIC GIFTS

There are four psychic abilities: clairvoyance, clairaudience (which includes mental telepathy), clairsentience, and clairgustance.

CLAIRVOYANCE

Psychic information can arrive in the form of pictures or visions, and *clairvoyance* is the gift of seeing these images. We all have an invisible third eye located in the middle of our forehead, which is sometimes referred to as the *psychic eye*. It's with this third eye that a clairvoyant "sees" information in the form of pictures, visions, or images.

1

When we see a ghost, a spirit guide, or a deceased loved one, that's also clairvoyance.

CLAIRAUDIENCE

Clairaudience is the gift of psychic hearing. This sounds simple enough, but it can become quite confusing. When a clairaudient receives information, it comes into his or her mind as thoughts. Since these thoughts don't sound any different than one's own thoughts, the clairaudient's job is to learn, through trial and error, to distinguish between personal thoughts and incoming psychic information (there's more on this in chapter 3).

There are a variety of sources that send thoughts to us; which sources we hear has a lot to do with the path we're on. We could be receiving information from our spirit guides, a guardian angel, deceased loved ones, or earthbound spirits. Spirits do not have voices as we do. The way they communicate with each other and with us is by projecting thoughts.

There's a great line in the Steven Spielberg movie *Always* that describes clairaudience. The character played by Richard Dreyfus is killed in a plane crash, and Audrey Hepburn, who plays an angel, has to explain to him that he's now a spirit guide to another character in the movie. She tells him that the way to communicate with human beings is to send thoughts to them. She says something like, "They always think it's their own thoughts, but that doesn't matter as long as they get the message." This is how our spirit guides and deceased loves ones communicate with us. They send us thoughts to give us guidance. Our souls know where the information is coming from, but we don't become conscious of the true source until we start paying more attention.

One of my favorite aspects of clairaudience is *mental telepathy*. This is "hearing" the thoughts of people who are either in your general vicinity or simply in your life. It's not uncommon for us to pick up the thoughts of people we are very connected to on a psychic level. My son, with whom I share a very strong psychic connection, can be making ribs for dinner in Lincoln, Nebraska, and I can be sitting in my office in Minneapolis thinking about and smelling ribs. Or one of my best friends who lives in California can be fighting the urge to have a hot fudge sundae, and I'll get in my car and go get one.

How many times have you verbalized a thought only to have someone you're with say she or he was just thinking the same thing? Has the thought of someone ever popped into your head and then the phone rang and it was that person? These are simply thoughts that people are sending out. They're thinking of us, and we receive these thoughts on a psychic level without being aware of it. As we grow psychically and spiritually, we become more open to mental telepathy, and it makes life pretty fun.

CLAIRSENTIENCE

The next psychic gift, *clairsentience*, has to do with sensing. This is more of a body feeling or sensing than actually seeing visions with your third eye or psychically hearing thoughts or voices. If someone is clairsentient, he or she has psychic radar working all the time, psychically feeling the environment as he or she goes through the day.

The blue lobster I have in my aquarium at home is a lot like a clairsentient. He has long tentacles that reach out in front of his body to scope out the environment as he moves through the tank. Clairsentients have this kind of sensing going on in their bodies. They can walk into a room or a meeting and sense the mood. I believe all psychics have this gift and use it their whole lives. It's how we survive living in these sensitive bodies. When we go into any situation, we send out our feelers because we want to know what kind of environment we're stepping into.

The downside to clairsentience is that we can become psychic sponges. We can soak up too much of the environment and carry it with us. I will cover this in more detail in chapter 2 and give some suggestions for how to create the necessary boundaries and distance yourself.

CLAIRGUSTANCE

Clairgustance is the last psychic gift, and it's an odd one. It's the gift of smell. People with clairgustance have a psychic nose, which means they smell things that aren't physically present. For example, one day a client asked me about a used car she was thinking of purchasing. She wanted to know if I felt there was anything wrong with it. I got the strong odor of an overheated engine. Despite this indication of potential trouble, she purchased the car anyway, and as it turned out, she continually had a problem with the engine overheating.

The most common way that clairgustance manifests itself is when a deceased loved one comes to visit us. The person will project a scent to us, and we'll find ourselves thinking about it, such as the cologne the person used to wear or anything else that immediately brings the loved one to mind. Once I was doing a reading for a woman, and I got the strong aroma of freshly baked bread. Then I had a psychic image of a woman on the other side, waving and smiling. She was wearing an apron, and I saw a picture of an oven. Again I got the smell of bread. I asked my client if freshly baked bread and a woman smiling and waving on the other side was significant to her, and she told me her aunt had just died and that when she was alive, she always baked bread for people. This was simply her aunt's way of saying hello.

The scent that is sensed during an experience of clairgustance doesn't last long. Usually a quick whiff is received, and then it's gone.

Do all psychics have all of these abilities? I think we all have clairsentience, but of the other gifts, most psychics have either clairvoyance or clairaudience, though some have both. Clairgustance is less common. The simplest way that a person can tell which abilities she or he has is by paying attention to the type of information that comes in throughout the day: is it in the form of thoughts, pictures, sensing, or smells? I encourage my beginning students to explore figuring out which gifts they possess.

HOW PSYCHIC GIFTS WORK

One of the most widespread misunderstandings about psychic gifts is how they work. People generally assume that psychics receive information as if it were a well-written telegram; unfortunately, it doesn't work that way. Clairvoyants, for example, get their information in the form of pictures, images, or visions. Their job is to interpret the pictures accurately, and to do this they must ask questions. Often, professional psychics need help from the clients themselves to properly interpret what the pictures mean. This has led skeptics to claim that psychics don't do anything other than fish for information and then give that information back to the client. What may look like "fishing" to an observer is simply part of the psychic's effort to be as accurate as possible in his or her interpretation.

People often ask me why it is that psychic information doesn't come in clear, laid-out sentences, and all I can tell them is that I wonder about this myself. When spirits communicate to us, they keep it brief and to the point. They don't embellish. Often, information comes in like words in a crossword puzzle, and if we get one word at a time, on its own, it might not mean much at first. We patiently wait for more information to come so we can put the whole message together.

Here's an example: I had a client who had been looking at various office spaces around town to rent. She didn't know which one to rent and asked if I could help her out. I got a picture of an O. I waited for another picture, but nothing else came. I asked her if O meant anything to her. Did any of the building names start with an O? No, not that she could remember. I asked my spirit guides the question again, and I got another O. There was absolutely no other information coming, so I turned to my intuition for help, which I often do when interpreting pictures. I asked my intuition if the O was significant. The response was *yes*. Thinking that perhaps O meant zero, or that nothing she'd seen so far was right, I asked my intuition if the building she was supposed to rent was among the buildings she had looked at. Again I felt a yes response, so that was not the answer.

Since my client and I were both stuck and unable to interpret the O, I dropped it and moved on to other questions she wanted me to address. After getting clear answers for all of those, I went back to the O and asked again what it meant. A thought (clairaudience) came into my head that said *full circle*. I asked my intuition if this meant she was supposed to go back to the original building she had looked at, and it gave me a strong nudge of *yes*. When I said this to my client, she told me that she had looked at that space several times, and she was hoping that we would confirm that she was on the right track!

I think the only way we're going to move away from thinking of psychics as entertaining fortune-tellers is by learning how these gifts work. My repeat clients see their readings with me as a partnership. We work together to unravel some of the goofy pictures I receive so that they can get all the information they need in order to move forward in their lives. They are not looking to be entertained or to have me prove that psychic gifts actually work. They have gotten to the stage where they want to work together with me to solve problems or heal themselves. And I really believe that's how it's supposed to be.

HOW THESE GIFTS WORK TOGETHER

Two popular television shows have been hosted by very gifted psychic mediums, John Edward's *Crossing Over* and *Beyond* with James Van Praagh. The work of both of these men exemplifies how psychic abilities work together. For those of you who have never seen these shows, I'll describe how the abilities work in concert.

A TV psychic begins by standing in the middle of the set, waiting for a strong pull (clairsentience). This pull would feel like a sudden energy running from the psychic to the person meant to get the reading. If this person were on the left side of the room, the psychic would turn in that direction and feel the connection grow stronger, perhaps getting an image of a male energy (clairvoyance). He or she might see the word *brother* (clairvoyance), or the feeling of brother might come (clairsentience). Then the psychic might get a picture of an elm tree, along with an image of a mallard duck (clairvoyance). Then the name *Don* might come in as a thought (clairaudience).

If the psychic were in a private session and not on TV, she or he would have time to wait for more pictures to come and possibly put the whole message together by her- or himself. But on television, the producers don't want any dead-air time, so the psychic has to move quickly. Once the psychic has an adequate amount of information, he or she will start asking questions, saying something like, "I'm feeling a connection to someone on the left side of the audience. I'm feeling a brother. Who has a deceased brother with a connection to an elm tree? I'm also seeing a mallard duck. . . . The name *Don* is coming to me. There's a significance to the color yellow. . . . Does any of this mean anything to someone on the left side of the audience?"

At this point, the psychic may not know whether Don is the deceased person or the person in the audience. As the psychic waits for someone in the audience to respond, she or he is also waiting for the deceased loved one to give more information. At the same time, the psychic knows the producers are watching the clock and also that there are other deceased loved ones waiting to get their turn to speak. In the space of thirty seconds or a minute, the psychic must interpret all the information as accurately as possible.

Usually it doesn't take long before someone in the audience responds. For instance, a woman wearing a yellow blouse might raise her hand and say she has a deceased brother named Don who collected replicas of mallard ducks. The psychic, not wanting to make a mistake, will ask what might be significant about an elm tree, and the woman might say, "We lived on Elm Street." Now that the psychic knows whom the message is for, he or she would tune in to the deceased person to see if there is a specific message for this person and pass this on. The psychic would then step back, clear the deceased person's energy from her or his mind, and ask for the next spirit to move forward.

I would love it if the information came in like a telegram: "Hello, my name is Don. My sister, Velma, is sitting on the left side of the audience in a yellow blouse. We used to live on Elm Street, and when I was living, I collected mallard ducks. Please tell my sister I'm doing great, as are Mom and Dad, who are both with me. Tell her we love her." But that isn't how it happens. Instead, the information arrives in shorthand: brother, sister, yellow, elm, ducks, happy.

WHERE DOES THE INFORMATION COME FROM?

Psychic information can come from several sources. Our spirit guides and guardian angels bring us information, and they get information on other people by communicating either with those people's guides or with their souls. Sometimes our deceased loved ones bring information, as do the deceased loved ones of the people we're reading. Earthbound spirits (ghosts) make feeble attempts at sending messages to us, and of course God gives us messages for ourselves and others.

In the beginning of my psychic development, I never knew who was giving me the information. The Ouija board spelled out grand names such as Zoltar and Unonden, and the voices said they were very high spiritual guides. But the quality of the messages wasn't congruent with a high master teacher or guide. After initially grabbing my interest, their messages turned toward the negative and the dramatic, such as "So-and-so is sick and will die soon," or "Your friend John will die in a car accident." Looking back, I now know that these were earthbound spirits, or ghosts, trying to mess with my head, but at the time I didn't know how to discern between correct messages and false ones.

The psychic information we receive for people comes from many different sources, and it is important to discern where it's coming from. Don't be naive about the spirits who will communicate with you, since some will indeed give you bad or hurtful information. Most people in the beginning of their development attract earthbound spirits because both parties are so eager to communicate. Whenever you open up to do psychic work, you need to ask your guides for help and make it clear (by stating it out loud) that you want no earthbound spirits channeling any information.

Eventually you'll be able to tell by the quality of the information if it's coming from a guide or a ghost. As you grow psychically, this gets easier because you'll know the feel of your guides versus other spirits around you. You'll be able to feel if the source of the information is a positive, clear, detached soul, or if the source has a hidden agenda, such as a deceased loved one trying to control someone's life.

ASKING FOR ACCURACY AND THANKING OUR GUIDES

I've never met a true psychic who wasn't conscientious about accuracy. No one wants to give misleading information. For one thing, the psychic's reputation is at

stake; no one's going to return to a psychic who repeat-
edly gives misinformation. Unfortunately, though, I know
there have been times when I unintentionally gave a
client incorrect information simply because I misinterpreted what I was seeing.

Before I begin a reading, I ask God to work through
me and give me clear, accurate information that will
help the client understand him- or herself better. I ask
for help with interpreting the visions accurately and hearing my guides clearly. I always thank God and my guides
before the information begins to flow, and then I focus on
the white light within my solar plexus (the area above the
belly button) and wait for the information to come.

We should always remember that we're not doing
this alone. We are relying on outside help, so I think it's
important to acknowledge and thank our guides. And
always, always pray for accuracy.

How do you feel about developing your psychic abilities? What are your expectations and goals? What are
your fears?

CHAPTER 2

PSYCHIC DEVELOPMENT PRELIMINARIES

In this section, I offer some strategies that are helpful to know before you begin developing your psychic gifts. I also cover how to live in this world with your psychic abilities and how to avoid some common pitfalls.

KEEP A PSYCHIC JOURNAL

Something I've found very helpful for anyone hoping to develop their psychic abilities, but especially for those having difficulties, is journaling. Journaling about the different stages of your development will help you sort everything out. For example, recording mental telepathy will help build your confidence in your clairaudient ability. And if you're feeling blocked or anxious, if old fears crop up, if past-life memories come to the surface regarding these abilities, or if you have nightmares about these abilities, writing them down will help tremendously. It's very beneficial to get all your feelings out on paper so that they don't block your progress.

Use the journaling space in this book to record all of your thoughts, feelings, fears, blocks, anticipations, expectations, and visions as you progress. I encourage you to do this every day.

KEEP YOUR LIFE IN BALANCE

If you are new to psychic phenomena and just discovering your own abilities, I want to caution you about something that I think is pretty common: getting totally swept up in the psychic world. My mom and I went through this ourselves.

In the fall of 1965, something very unusual happened to my family. One of my brothers had the terrifying experience of seeing a white figure floating through a room. Since we were mainstream Presbyterians, we had no idea what to make of this, so Mom called around to some of her friends to see if anyone could refer her to a psychic. She got the name and number of a psychic/medium living in St. Paul, Minnesota, and she gave her a call. The psychic said that this had happened for a reason, that Mom and all four of us kids had some unusual gifts, and that she wanted to see Mom and her oldest daughter for a psychic reading. Mom's immediate response was that we needed to think it over, and she told the psychic that we'd get back to her. By the next day, Mom and I were so curious about what the woman had said that Mom called her back and scheduled appointments for both of us.

I was seventeen years old and very nervous about seeing a psychic. I had no idea what to expect and assumed she would be the stereotypical gypsy fortune-teller — toothless, with gold hoop earrings and long dangling scarves, staring into a crystal ball or reading our palms. I was pleasantly surprised to find just the opposite. Mrs. Olson was a very sweet, gentle woman from England. She looked like she belonged behind the counter in a library rather than in a carnival sideshow. I wondered if she would know all my deep, dark secrets and when I was going to die, but as it turned out, she knew neither. Instead, she told me that I had been born with psychic abilities and the gift of healing. She said that I had come here to this lifetime to develop my abilities and then to teach others how to develop theirs.

After that, in the beginning of my mother's and my development, we thought that every light that flickered and every noise the house made were communications from the spirit world. We bought a Ouija board, thinking it would hasten our psychic development. We read whatever we could find about "the occult," which is what it was called back in the sixties. We became completely consumed in developing our psychic abilities and shut out the rest of the world. We went from one end of the spectrum to the other, from having no involvement in any of this to totally immersing ourselves in it.

However, this type of behavior can lead you to burn out quickly. In a few cases I've watched frustrated students go overboard and then decide to completely close the door on their abilities. My advice is to take it slow and get into all of this in moderation. Continue to live your life the way you did before you got involved in psychic development. Maintain a balance in your life so that you don't burn out. Ultimately, developing your psychic abilities is about being on a spiritual journey and developing your spiritual gifts. It is about a way of living and seeing, and you must remember to stay grounded in your physical life here on Earth.

PROTECT YOUR FRIENDSHIPS

In the beginning of your development, you'll probably be practicing on willing friends, and it'll be fun. Lots of sharing and lots of laughs.

Then a common problem will slowly creep in: over time, your friends may start looking to you for guidance on everything in their lives. Whenever anything comes up that causes them anxiety, fear, or pain of some kind, they'll want you to tell them the outcome. Your friendships will no longer have the same give and take. You may start to feel it is all give, give, give on your part, and you eventually might find yourself avoiding your friends altogether.

Another problem might come up when you go to parties. If word has gotten out that you've developed your psychic abilities, people will come up to you at parties and ask if they can "just ask one question." This might seem fun at first, but it gets old very quickly.

My advice is to nip this in the bud. Let your friends know that when you're out socializing with them, you're there to have a good time like everyone else. Tell them to call you at a more appropriate time with their questions. Or get some business cards made up. Then, when people approach you for some free psychic advice, hand them your business card and tell them to call to set up an appointment.

I know this sounds cold and off-putting, but this is the kind of thing that causes us to burn out. Everyone in the world has some kind of problem, and everyone wants to know how it's going to turn out. If you let yourself become the psychic ATM machine for everyone you know, you will come to resent them *and* your gifts.

You need to decide what you're willing to do and then set boundaries and stick to them. There will be times when your intuition is really pushing you to give someone a message, and other times you will get a definite feeling to stay out of it. Follow your intuition in these cases, not your intellect. In the long run, though, just remember that by protecting yourself, you are also protecting your friendships.

DETACH YOURSELF

Whenever new students tell me they can't wait to develop their abilities so that they can help people, I get concerned, because caring too much can actually get in the way of being a good psychic.

There are two kinds of caregivers in the world, and many well-intentioned people don't know the difference. Unhealthy caregivers come from a needy place. They help others in order to feel good about themselves and because they want people to like them. Oftentimes, they set up situations where people must rely on them so they will continue to be needed.

Healthy caregivers don't have a personal agenda other than to assist others in whatever they're going through. Healthy caregivers detach their emotions so that they can give the person they're helping whatever that person needs. Healthy caregivers learn to let go of their expectations concerning the outcome of the information they receive. This doesn't mean you can't be loving or caring; it just means keeping your own needs in check and understanding that you can truly heal only yourself, not others.

Psychics, especially, need to learn to become healthy caregivers. Psychics who get into this work to save the world soon develop a savior complex, and invariably they burn out fast and are ineffective.

In order to be effective, we have to keep ourselves

out of the readings when we're doing them. Detachment is very important when giving psychic information. It's tough delivering bad news to people, and there is always the temptation to fudge the truth in order to spare feelings. And yet it's unhealthy to deliver good news if it's not true. I've met psychics who give cheerful, positive readings so that their clients will feel good and keep coming back, but what these psychics fail to realize (though eventually they get it) is that if the information isn't accurate, the clients aren't going to return. More important, however, the client will believe and act on this false information, leading to potentially more pain and problems when events don't come to pass as expected.

We are the messengers, the channels that the information comes through. We can deliver that information in a loving, caring way, but we must remember not to get involved in the situations of others in order to help them fix their problems. That's their responsibility.

RESPECT BOUNDARIES

As psychics, it's very important that we respect people's privacy. When I do readings for people, I always ask them what areas of their lives they want me to look at. I get very specific because I'm not going to look at something the person doesn't want me to. If a woman asks me to look at her marriage, I ask her what areas of her marriage she wants me to focus on. If a man asks about his health, I ask if there's a specific area of his body he's concerned about. Some people tell me to just go ahead and tell them whatever I see, but I won't do this. The client has to direct me, or I won't go there, and the reason is simple.

When I first started giving psychic readings, I read things about people that I assumed they wanted to know about, but that wasn't always the case. People would get upset and tell me that they hadn't wanted me to go *there*. Health problems, marital infidelity, financial concerns — you may consider the information important or harmless, but you have no way of knowing for sure, so it's best to have the client direct the reading. We need to respect each person's personal boundaries.

Another thing that pops up a lot in psychic readings is that people will ask you to read private information about someone else in their life. Humans are inherently curious about each other; in almost every reading I do, the client asks about some other person in his or her life, whether it's a significant other, a parent, a child, a boss, a co-worker, an employee, a neighbor, or a recent acquaintance. Sometimes we psychics can get information for people regarding their relationships, and sometimes we can't. When someone asks for this kind of information, the psychic is the one who has to set the boundaries and let the person know if giving this information doesn't feel right. Otherwise, you are putting yourself in the position of violating someone else's personal boundaries without consent.

For these reasons — and I can't emphasize this strongly enough — it's essential to approach your work with integrity. But the other reason why it's so important to respect others' boundaries and privacy is karma. Karma is the Golden Rule in action; it basically means that whatever you do to someone else will be done to you. If you violate someone's privacy, your privacy will be violated in one way or another. It's that simple! From a karmic standpoint, you want to remember that all of your actions are recorded in your soul. If you abuse others with your psychic abilities by revealing things they don't want to know about themselves or revealing things about third parties — let alone by scamming them, trying to control or manipulate them, or lying to them so that somehow you'll benefit — *you* will eventually pay the consequences because of it. The law of karma applies to everyone.

STAY GROUNDED

One of the definite disadvantages of being psychic is that we can get pretty spacey and feel completely ungrounded. This happens because we're opening ourselves up to different dimensions of reality, and the higher up we go, the spacier we can feel. As we continue to grow psychically, we have longer communications with our guides, and deeper meditations, which can make us feel very light indeed.

To ground yourself, you can do basically anything that reminds you that you are living in a human body on this planet. Getting in contact with the earth itself is very effective. Whatever you do, make sure it engages as many of your senses as possible: touch, taste, smell, hearing, and sight. The more senses you have going, the more grounded you'll feel.

Here are some specific recommendations for grounding yourself:

1. Exercise. It awakens your body. And while exercising, you have to stay mentally in your body if for no other reason than to avoid dropping weights on your foot or flying off the treadmill.

2. Eat a meal with heavy foods, such as meat, potatoes, chocolate, oatmeal, and so on. Choose whatever gives your stomach that full feeling.

3. Go to places with lots of people and other stimuli. For me, after doing an intense reading or several in one day, sometimes the best thing I can do for myself is to go to a shopping mall or a supermarket and walk around.

I take in all the colors and smells and stay very conscious of where I am. (However, some psychics find malls the opposite of grounding, so you'll have to try it and see if it works for you.)

4. Take a shower or a bath to help you get focused. *Feel the water* on your body.

5. Watch a movie that gets you into your feelings, such as laughter, sadness, joy, or anger; experiencing these emotions can help you feel grounded.

6. Go outdoors and experience nature. Touch the trees, the grass, the dirt. Feel the sun. Breathe the fresh air and smell the flowers.

7. Carry rocks in your pockets.

8. Make love. Sex will keep you in your body and focused on being here (as long as it is not abusive sex).

9. Engage in a favorite hobby or any manual activity that requires your concentration.

10. Avoid working at a computer — this is not very grounding. If you have to work on a computer and you're feeling spacey, be sure to get up and do something physical from time to time.

11. Play music, sing, or dance. All of these activities are very grounding.

12. Try this visualization: imagine roots coming out of the bottom of your feet and going deep into the earth. This will help you feel more anchored.

When I need to feel more grounded, I plan to . . .

_____

_____

_____

_____

_____

_____

_____

_____

_____

_____

_____

_____

_____

_____

AVOID BEING A PSYCHIC SPONGE

Another downfall of being psychic is that you're more sensitive to people and the world around you. Oftentimes, you will feel people's emotional, mental, and physical pain simply by thinking of them or being around them. Because of this level of sensitivity, you will have to make a concentrated effort to protect yourself so that you can function in the world as normally as possible.

The one psychic ability that can be particularly bothersome is clairsentience, or the gift of sensing. There's a fine line between using clairsentience to read people or situations and becoming a "psychic sponge." Psychic sponges literally soak up the emotional or physical feelings of the people around them and sometimes even of the world in general. If you are not sure whether you are one of these people who picks up everyone else's "stuff," answer the following questions:

- After spending five minutes with a crabby friend, do you feel crabby?

- After having a quick conversation with your boss, who happens to have a headache, do you end up with a headache?

- If you visit a neighbor who's suffering from depression, do you walk away feeling depressed?

- Have you ever run into a friend at the grocery store who was very angry over something, and then you wound up feeling angry for the rest of the day?

If any of these describes you, the good news is that you have clairsentience. The bad news is that you are unwittingly soaking up everyone else's feelings and acting like a psychic sponge.

Have no fear. Help is on the way. I have a couple of simple tips that will protect you from soaking up everyone else's vibes. The number one suggestion is... buy some sponges! I'm serious about this.

I have a dear friend who is the quintessential psychic sponge (as are many of my students), and she was affected by it in all areas of her life. She was always soaking up so much random energy that she had a hard time discerning whether she was feeling her own emotions or someone else's. I gave her the clearing exercise (which I'll describe in a moment), but it wasn't enough. One day in meditation I asked my inner voice what would be helpful for her. The message came to send her sponges that she could put around her house — one by her phone, so that whenever she was talking to someone, the sponge would soak up the energy coming from the other end of the line; one by her computer to soak up the energy coming from her screen; one by her front door to soak up the energy of people who came to visit; one in her car to absorb the energy she would pick up from other drivers; one by her bed so that she could get a good night's sleep. My guides even suggested she put a small piece of a sponge inside her bra or pocket. Finally, they told me that once a week, if not more often, she should clear the sponges by rinsing them in water that contained sea salt.

I mailed her some sponges along with the above instructions, and she noticed that having the sponges around visibly reminded her to do the clearing exercise as well. She began doing this on a regular basis, and it made a big difference in her life. She is no longer soaking up everyone else's energy and no longer feels like she's bouncing off the walls with so much scattered energy in her body. It's made it a lot easier for her to distinguish her own feelings.

If you feel you're as sensitive as my friend, I strongly suggest that you buy some sponges and put them around your home and office. As goofy as this sounds, it really is a simple, effective little tool. Then, once or twice a week, put one teaspoon of sea salt in two cups of water and soak the sponges in this water. As the sponges are soaking, simply ask the universe to clear all the negative energy from them. Then rinse them out and put them back where you had them.

STAY AWAY FROM DRUGS
AND ALCOHOL

I would suggest not doing psychic exercises when you've been doing drugs or drinking. Psychically gifted people are very sensitive as it is, and adding mind-altering chemicals can leave you very vulnerable. It's true that some mind-altering experiences can be quite interesting, to say the least. But when you're under the influence, you run the risk of attracting "undesirables" to you, such as earthbound spirits who were addicted to drugs or alcohol when they were living. This is the last thing you need. For more information, I suggest picking up copies of my books *Relax, It's Only a Ghost* and *Dear Echo* and reading about possession.

If you have a serious problem with alcohol or drugs, you really shouldn't be opening yourself up psychically at all, since you could be inviting a variety of psychic experiences that you might not be able to deal with. Wait until you're committed to sobriety and have laid a spiritual foundation for yourself. Then you'll be more equipped to handle whatever comes along.

WAIT FOR SUNNY SKIES

For the first couple years of your development, I strongly suggest that you don't open up psychically if you're experiencing bad weather or if it's predicted for that day. Low or high barometric pressure can make us feel off-center or spacier than normal — talk about feeling ungrounded! We can easily pick up the energy in the atmosphere, and depending upon what's going on, it can make us feel very distracted. If there's a lot of intense energy, like tornado weather, we can feel it in our bodies, and it can feel like a caged lion. When you're experiencing intense weather, I strongly recommend that you try one of the three psychic protection exercises that follow (Clear Bubble, Eggshell, or Purple Cape), so that the weather won't affect you as much.

PROTECT YOURSELF PSYCHICALLY

Are you one of those people who has a tough time being in public because the vibes are so intense? Here are some more suggestions for how you can protect yourself psychically.

EXERCISE: CLEARING

My guides have told me that all people go through their days picking up energy from other people, and that at the end of each day, our auras (the energy fields around our bodies) look like decorated Christmas trees. They said in order for us to feel clear, we need to clear our auras on a regular basis, kind of like running the lint remover over our clothes.

This clearing exercise is very effective for all psychics, whether clairsentient or not. Get into the habit of doing it throughout your day and before crawling into bed. If necessary, write it down on a piece of paper and carry it with you. Get in the habit of saying it whenever you're feeling kind of off.

To begin, close your eyes and take a couple of nice, relaxing breaths. Then simply ask God or the universe to clear you:

> Please clear my mind.
> Clear my mind.
> Please clear my body.
> Clear my body.
> Please clear my soul.
> Clear my soul.
> Please clear me psychically.
> Clear me psychically.

You can also be more specific, adding any or all of the following anytime you want:

Please clear my home.
Clear my home.
Please clear my work area.
Clear my work area.
Please clear my bed.
Clear my bed.
(Or, clear my car, clear my pet, and so on.)

You should notice a change right away. I tell my students the first night of class that even if they decide not to develop their abilities and never come back to class, I want them to always do the clearing exercise because it's so helpful for anyone living on this planet. You don't have to be a psychic sponge to pick up other people's energy, and it can be a real burden if you don't know what to do about it.

EXERCISE: CLEAR BUBBLE

Using your imagination, visualize yourself surrounded by a bubble of strong see-through polyurethane, like an adult-size ziplock baggie with the zipper zipped up! Get in the habit of visualizing this whenever you leave the house, and you'll be surprised at how much more you can do without being psychically or physically affected by it. If you're claustrophobic, this is a good exercise for you; since you can see through the bubble, you won't feel confined.

EXERCISE: EGGSHELL

Whenever you're feeling especially vulnerable, I suggest visualizing yourself surrounded by a shell, such as an eggshell with no cracks or holes in it. This seems to be even more protective than the invisible bubble because on a psychic level you're putting up a very visible shield that separates you from others.

EXERCISE: PURPLE CAPE

This visualization has come to me in many of the meditations I've done for my students regarding psychic protection. Using your imagination, visualize a floor-length purple cape with a hood on it; the inside lining of the cape is turquoise. Visualize putting the cape on and zipping up the front. Purple is a very strong, protective color that is heavier and therefore more grounding, and turquoise is very similar but with a lighter vibration. The combination of these two colors is very good protection, so whenever you're feeling vulnerable, visualize wearing this cape.

CHAPTER 3

UNDERSTANDING PSYCHIC INFORMATION

As you begin to open up to and receive psychic information, you will need to learn how to distinguish between your own thoughts and any voices coming in, and how to recognize and interpret visions you may receive. Opening up, receiving, and interpreting are what this chapter is all about.

LEARNING TO RECEIVE

One bit of advice I have for those who are just beginning is this: wear the information you receive like a loose garment. Until you learn more about interpretation and the various forms of psychic information, don't take anything you receive too seriously. Remember, you're still in training!

In the beginning of your development, focus simply on learning how to receive the thoughts and pictures coming into your psychic center, and worry about understanding them later. Before you begin doing psychic readings, you need to open up your third eye and psychic ears, and you need to learn how to get yourself out of the way. Here are some tips for doing just that.

PRACTICE WITH A PARTNER YOU TRUST

Every beginner struggles with the fear of being wrong. You get past that fear by practicing with a partner who you know will be supportive. It's important that your partner be a person you trust — you're going to be taking a lot of risks with this person, and you don't want to have to worry about being criticized. In chapter 4, I provide you with four exercises for practicing; all of them require working with a trusted partner.

TELL YOUR PARTNER EVERYTHING

When I was just beginning to develop my own abilities, the first time I ever did one of these exercises (the Psychometry exercise on page 105) in a class, my partner gave me a fountain pen. I held it in my hand, and into my head came a picture of a bag of apples. My first thought was to blow it off because it seemed so insignificant, and I didn't want to say anything stupid. Unfortunately, every time I concentrated on my third eye, I saw this bag of apples. Then I saw a porch with a rocking chair. My rational mind argued that these images had nothing to do with the pen, and so I discounted them.

When my teacher came over, she asked me what information I was getting. Because I didn't want to be laughed at, I told her I wasn't getting anything. She asked, "If you're not seeing anything, what's that bag of apples?" It totally freaked me out. She said that I had to tell my partner *everything* I was seeing and feeling because this was the only way I was going to learn how to discern between psychic information and my own random thoughts. She also said I had to get my ego out of the way and stop worrying about being wrong. For me, this was a whole lot easier said than done. I shared with my partner the images that were coming to me: the bag of apples, a porch with a rocking chair, and an apple orchard. He said that the pen had belonged to his grandfather, who owned an apple orchard and used to sit in his rocking chair on the front porch of his farm and look out over his apple trees. I was blown away. I was also grateful that my teacher had pushed me to say the things I was seeing, hearing, and feeling.

Since I can't be there to push you, you are going to have to push yourself. Tell your partner everything, all of the images, thoughts, and feelings that come to you. Be willing to be completely wrong (again, this is why it's important to work with someone you trust). This is the only way you will be able to learn what accurate information feels like.

There are also practical reasons for you to say everything you're seeing as it happens. One is that sometimes no new information will come until you've given the person what you've already received. Another is that sometimes the information comes very fast, and you must quickly relate what you're seeing in order to keep up with it. If you're too busy thinking about what's happening and let your ego and fears of being wrong get in the way, you might miss important information.

LEARN TO DISCERN

Clairaudience is the gift of hearing, and this means that spirit communicates to us through thought. It would be fairly easy to understand and interpret these thoughts if they sounded like distinct voices, but they don't. Spirits' thoughts sound similar to our own, and so it takes time to develop the ability to distinguish between the two. Learning how to do this requires you to take some risks, because when a thought pops into your head, you'll have to run it by the person you're practicing with to see if it's a clairaudient message or one of your thoughts. I guarantee that if you really work at learning how to discern one from the other, before long you'll be able to do so.

FOCUS ON SIMPLE OBJECTS

When I was growing up, I thought crystal balls and tea leaves had psychic information inside and that when a gypsy gazed into these things, she or he was creating amazing pictures that foretold someone's future. Even though this didn't make logical sense to me, I couldn't figure out where else the information could be coming from. It never occurred to me that these objects were simply a focal point allowing physical eyes to focus on something while psychic pictures came into the gypsy's third eye.

When I finally grasped how clairvoyance works, I realized that the crystal ball or the tea leaves could just as well be a hockey puck or a jar of peanut butter. As you practice receiving clairvoyant images, choose some simple object for your physical eyes to focus on so that you won't get distracted by your surroundings. Staring at a wall or the floor or keeping your eyes closed all work equally well.

INTERPRETING WHAT YOU SEE

Perhaps the most important part of giving psychic information is how we're interpreting what we're seeing. I believe we get the information accurately, but it's how we interpret the information that can make or break a psychic message for someone.

INTUITION, YOUR GREATEST HELPER

Using your intuition is a very important part of your psychic development and your psychic work. Your intuition will always let you know if you're on the right track with your interpretation of psychic information. I always rely on my inner voice when doing a reading. If I get a picture I can't interpret, I go right to my intuition and start asking it questions: Is this how I should interpret the picture? What does this mean? I ask my intuition for clarity all the time.

Here's one of my goofy little pictures for you. Imagine the pit in a peach. Now imagine having one of those deep inside your soul. Within that seed is a silent voice of truth and clarity; this voice speaks to us more through an inner knowing than with an actual voice. You know that feeling you get in your gut when you just *know* something? You just knew a certain someone was going to call, or you just knew that you should've turned left instead of right? This silent voice of knowing is your intuition, and it comes from the divine within you. This inner knowing will never lie to you, and its guidance is 100 percent accurate.

When it comes to interpreting psychic information accurately, intuition will be your best helper. I can't say enough about the accuracy and integrity that intuition will bring to your work. It will help you not only as a psychic but in every area of your life. If you're already accustomed to living by this inner voice, you know just how helpful it can be. If this whole concept is new to you, I suggest getting a copy of my book *A Still, Small Voice: A Psychic's Guide to Awakening Intuition*.

PSYCHIC VISION, FEAR, OR EGO?

Often when people are just developing their psychic abilities, they haven't learned how to distinguish between a true vision, a fear, or a picture that their ego might be creating, and this can be very frightening. Students often tell me about previous experiences when they thought they were receiving an intuitive message or a psychic prediction only to find out it was one of their fears or it was their ego wanting to impress someone with psychic information.

I want you to think about what fear feels like. It's usually located in the stomach area, and it has a strong energy to it — it's that sinking feeling in the pit of your stomach that spreads quickly throughout your whole body. Sometimes people mistake this feeling for intuition because both feelings are located in the same area, but the feeling of fear does *not* indicate your intuition. Intuition does not have any emotion attached to it. It simply gives us information. As for the ego, it likes to be the hero, so from time to time it might try to come up with psychic information in order to bedazzle people.

To help you understand which of the three your vision might be, first do the Clearing exercise (page 33) to help you clear the information from your head and the fear from your body. Ask yourself how the information came to you. Did it simply pop into your head out of nowhere? If so, then it might have been a true vision, but also ask yourself, is it related to anything you might have seen on TV or in the newspaper the day before? Did it feel fearful when you saw it in your mind? It's very important that you calm yourself down and determine the source of the information. Some of my students saw visions of airplanes going into buildings after the 9/11 terrorist attacks, and they thought that these were predictions of more attacks coming. But when I had them trace back the feelings associated with these visions, they discovered their fears were creating these pictures.

In a similar way, say you're planning to take a car trip, and the day before you leave, you get images of a car crash and everyone dying. The vision feels really scary, and afterward your body is racing with adrenaline. What have you just seen?

First things first, calm yourself down. Ask yourself, are these images similar to anything you've seen in the media lately? Has someone you know recently been in a wreck? The fact that the information came with an adrenaline rush of fear should tell you that this "vision" is connected to fears concerning the trip. If it was a psychic prediction, you would have been given the information without any emotion attached. You would have seen an accident (clairvoyance), thoughts would have come into your mind of the car breaking down (clairaudience), or you would have had an inner knowingness that something was wrong, a simple certainty that you weren't supposed to go on the trip (intuition). These would have all arrived as plain information. Another interesting distinction between real and manufactured visions is this: when our mind creates a vision, the images go on and on and seem to get more elaborate with time, whereas a psychic message comes quickly and is gone. My teacher always told us to pay attention when spirits speak because they don't repeat themselves!

In other words, here is what to look for:

- If it's a prophetic vision (even a negative one), it will simply be a picture that came in out of nowhere, with no emotion attached to it.

- If it's one of your fears, you'll be very aware of fear as you're seeing the pictures. They will seem to go hand in hand. Fear also multiplies quickly and can easily create a hundred scary scenarios in a matter of seconds, so beware.

- If it's a picture your ego has created (in its desire to experience a psychic vision), your mind will be racing with thoughts, and there will be mixed feelings of excitement and fear.

EXERCISE: ASK FOR THE TRUTH

One of the coolest things about our intuition is that it will show us the truth of any situation whenever we ask (so long as our agenda isn't in the way). If you've gotten some information and aren't sure what to do with it, try this visualization. This is a very good discipline to learn in any case because it is a simple technique that you will use over and over in your psychic work.

Find a quiet place away from the noises of the world and sit down. Close your eyes and take three or four relaxing breaths. Focus on the area of your solar plexus. Inside it is a white light at the center of your soul, the light of God within. Using your imagination, visualize this light and completely focus your attention on it. Take a few more relaxing breaths, and with each breath, imagine this light getting bigger and brighter until it completely surrounds you. Feel the peacefulness of the light.

Once your mind has calmed down, and you're able to focus only on this light, tell your inner voice to show you the truth of the situation. Ask it if the information that came to you is accurate. If it is, you'll get an inner knowing of *yes*. Then, while continuing to focus on the light, ask if there's anything you should do about it. If your mind starts to race with thoughts and ideas, return your focus to the calmness of the white light.

If the answer is no, you will either get a *no* feeling or it will feel blank. If that's the case, thank the light for guiding you and open your eyes when you feel done.

Some students protest that they aren't good at visualizing and they can't see this light, but hear me loud and clear: you have an imagination, and you can imagine this light. You're not making it up — we all have this light within our soul. You may have to use your imagination in the beginning to open your mind to this idea, but after you've done this a few times, it will become very natural to see the light inside.

USE YOUR JOURNAL

You may find that no answers come when you're doing the visualization above, but over the course of the next few days, more information may come when you least expect it. I would strongly suggest any time you get information and you're not sure what to do with it, record it in your psychic journal. You may indeed have picked up on an impending situation through your psychic abilities. But even if not, writing in your psychic journal can be very helpful. Recording the visions, thoughts, and intuitive feelings can help you sort through what's fact or fiction, ego or fear. You can review the things you've previously written and get a better understanding of the meaning of the pictures, images, and feelings you've received. This is how we learn to discern truth from nontruth, the feeling of accurate psychic information from the feeling of random thoughts, fearful imaginings, and self-created visions. This is how we establish accuracy.

Today when I practiced visualizing the white light at the center of my soul . . .

INTERPRETATION FOR CLAIRVOYANTS

Interpreting clairvoyant images gets easier the longer you work at it, so have patience. One way to think of it is that it is like reading a cartoon strip without any words. The pictures are sometimes literal (a man running up a hill means that the client is going to have to run up a hill) and other times symbolic (the client will have to work hard to achieve a goal). The clairvoyant's job is to interpret both.

Unlike dream books that interpret the pictures for us, there isn't any such book for clairvoyants because the pictures mean different things to different people. To help you understand this better, here are some examples of clairvoyant pictures, along with how those pictures might be interpreted:

1. A friend asks you whether or not he will get
    the job he just applied for. You open your third
    eye and see one or more of the following:

PICTURE	POSSIBLE INTERPRETATION
A door opening A paycheck Your friend wearing a new suit	A job opportunity coming
A door closing	No job opportunities at this time

Your friend reading
   the want ads
	Continuing to search; also
	   might indicate that the want
	   ads are how he will find
	   a job

A Mayflower truck	Moving; possibly a
	   relocation to accept
	   a job elsewhere

2. A client asks you to look at her health, specif-
    ically her lungs. Here are some pictures you
    might see:

PICTURE	POSSIBLE INTERPRETATION
Black coals in a chimney	Cancer
A clear day	Lungs are clear
Mold	Allergy to mold; or mold is what's causing the problem
Climbing up a very steep mountain	Difficulty breathing; or she has a long road ahead to restore health
A hospital	Will need medical care; or she should go to a hospital to get checked out
A coffin	She could be in the dying process
A clean bill of health The word *bronchitis* The word *asthma*	Self-explanatory
Lots of water or an overflowing river	Lungs are full of liquid or filling up with liquid

3. A friend asks how long it's going to be before
    he meets Ms. Right. Here are some pictures
    that relate to timing:

PICTURE	POSSIBLE INTERPRETATION
Snow on the ground	Winter
Colored leaves on trees	Autumn
Little buds on trees	Spring
A calendar with the first initial of the month, such as *A*	A month beginning with that letter; that is, April or August
Fireworks going off	July
A number, such as 3	This could mean the third month (March), or 3 days, 3 weeks, 3 months, or 3 years from now; ask your intuition for help discerning the truth
An astrological sign	The month of that sign
Someone standing in the way	There's someone he needs to deal with before he can meet Ms. Right

4. The same friend asks you to describe Ms. Right, and here are some of the pictures you might get:

PICTURE	POSSIBLE INTERPRETATION
The face of someone you know	Ms. Right will have qualities similar to this person
An old picture frame	Someone from the past
Someone tall or short Dark hair A runner or athlete	Self-explanatory
A doctor's coat	A medical professional
A teddy bear	A huggable, teddy-bear type
Stacks of books	Someone who likes to read; or an author, a librarian, a student, etc.
Fishing	Someone who likes to fish
A broken heart	Someone whose heart has recently been broken; or your friend's heart will be broken
An astrological sign	Ms. Right's sign; or Ms. Right has characteristics of this sign

KEEPING INTERPRETATION SIMPLE

When interpreting pictures, it is important to remember to look at the various meanings and their simplest forms. The guides are going to give you kindergarten-level pictures to make it as easy as possible for you to grasp the meaning of their messages. You might think, given the simple nature of these pictures, that you couldn't possibly misinterpret them. On the contrary, your intellect will often go in the opposite direction, looking for the most complicated interpretations. That's why you should run all your interpretations by your intuition, which will let you know if you're on the right track. Don't be in a hurry. Accuracy is everything.

RECEIVING PERSONAL SYMBOLS

When our guides answer a question about someone's personality, they sometimes give us a picture of someone else we know. This is their way of saying that the person in question has similar characteristics to the person we know. Using example 4 above, if your friend asked you to describe what his Ms. Right would be like, and you got an image of your neighbor Judy, it would mean that the woman would be similar in personality to Judy. Instead of giving you all kinds of different pictures to describe your friend's Ms. Right, your guides would be more efficient, using a shorthand they know you'll understand: Judy. Your job is to determine which of

Judy's characteristics are similar to Ms. Right's. These characteristics will usually be the first things you think of when you think of Judy — perhaps chatty, friendly, hard-worker, gardener, writer.

You'll need to ask your intuition for assistance in discerning which characteristics are accurate. Is Ms. Right chatty? *Yes*. Is she friendly? Strong *Yes*. Is she hard-working? *Yes*. Family oriented? *No*. A gardener? *Yes*. And so on.

PREDICTING TIMING

People ask timing questions (like the one in example 3 above) all the time: How soon will I meet my soul mate? When will I get married? When will I get a job? When should I go on vacation? When will my alcoholic spouse quit drinking? When will I get pregnant? When will my health improve? When will my sick parent die? Questions like these come up all the time, and our job is to pin our guides down to exact times.

Timing questions are always interesting, and tricky, because we're asking spirits who don't go by timing to put everything into our earthly time frame. They do the best they can, but getting them to be very specific isn't easy. When they give you a number, such as 2, 3, or 4, your job is to discern if that means hours, days, weeks, months, or years. Sometimes they'll give you a number, and when you ask for more information, they might give you a picture that represents a season, such as snow on the ground or colored leaves in the fall. If you get one of these season pictures, pay close attention to the details. Is there a lot of snow on the ground or just a little bit? Are the colored leaves on the trees or on the ground? Are the baby buds on the trees just coming out or are they ready to blossom? These details will help you fine-tune when the event will occur.

If you're clairaudient, you might hear the word *soon*, but don't take this at face value. Keep hunting for more specific information because *soon* to a spirit who lives without clocks and calendars could be tomorrow or ten years from now! I can't tell you the number of clients who have come back to me a year or two after their reading to tell me that everything that was predicted came true, but the timing was off.

PUTTING THE PIECES TOGETHER

A friend of mine who is in the process of opening up her third eye recently said that communicating with her guides is like playing charades. They give her a picture, and then she proceeds to play twenty questions with them in order to figure out what the picture means. I couldn't have said it better myself!

The more you practice asking questions, the more pictures you'll receive, and then it's like putting together the pieces to a jigsaw puzzle. Once you've done that, you'll need to discern if the pictures are real or symbolic, and again, you do this by enlisting the help of your intuition. It's pretty cool how it all comes together to create messages for people. Here are some examples of how entire messages get put together.

- A client wanted to know what the missing piece in her life was, and the image that came was of a woman walking up a rocky hillside trail in Peru in search of mystic monks. My job as the clairvoyant was to figure out if she was really supposed to go to Peru in search of these monks or if this was symbolic of her needing to go on a spiritual quest. I asked my guides, but they simply smiled at me and sent the thought that she'd know soon. I asked my intuition, but it didn't give me any specifics other than that the information was important for her to hear.

- Another client asked me why she felt so alone, and the image that came was of a woman living in a tree house. I saw people walking by but no one stopping to say hello. I also noticed that she never looked out the windows. She just sat in the middle of the tree house wondering why she was so alone. To interpret this, I asked the picture some questions. What did the tree house symbolize? Being away from society? *Yes*. Was this something she was creating? *Yes.* Why was she choosing this way of life? *Fear* was the answer that came into my head. Fear of people, fear of intimacy, fear of what? I asked. The statement that came into my head was *Yes, fear of everything. She isolates herself to protect herself.*

When I gave the client the information that she was the one creating the loneliness out of fear, she broke down crying and said she didn't know what to do about it. The next image that came into my head was an office with some-one sitting at a desk. I asked my intuition if this was a clergyperson and got no response. I asked if this was a counselor and got a strong intuitive feeling of *yes.* I asked if she knew this person yet, and I got a *no* feeling but heard the words *sister does.* I asked the woman if her sister was seeing a therapist, and she said that her sister's neighbor was a therapist. I asked my guides if this was who she should see about healing these fears, and they said *yes.*

• Another client asked me where she should move to, and I saw an image of a friend of mine who lives in Scottsdale, Arizona. I asked the client if Scottsdale was one of the places she was think-ing of moving to, and she said that Scottsdale was her first choice. (Some images are easier to figure out than others!)

- A client asked how soon it would be before he found a job. First, I got an image of a piggy bank full of money. The next image was of him holding it upside down and shaking out the last penny. Then I saw a picture of him sitting at a desk shuffling papers. After questioning my intuition, I interpreted this image sequence to mean that he would not get a job until he had used up all of his savings.

WHAT IF THE MESSAGES ARE WRONG?

At this point, it's important to address another confusing aspect of psychic readings. That is, why is it that information can sometimes be so off?

OUR SOUL'S PLAN

Sometimes, even when you are certain you are getting a psychic communication, and even when you've been thorough about confirming your interpretation of it, the information you receive will wind up being incorrect. It took me a long time to understand why this could be, since I believed that all psychic communications are true. At first I always assumed I had done something wrong. Instead, what I've come to learn is that most often our souls have plans for us that we aren't aware of, and they will sometimes give us false information if it moves us in the right direction.

For a long time, I looked at life only through my humanness and gave very little thought to my soul or "her plan." As I got more and more into my spiritual path and came to believe in reincarnation, I opened up to the idea that you could look at life through the soul's perspective, which is distinct from our conscious mind. When, as I progressed as a psychic, souls began choosing to communicate to me directly, I stumbled into an unexpected difficulty. It was challenging at times to find a way to tell a person's "body" or "conscious mind" information that his or her own soul was communicating to me, and even sometimes withholding from me. Here's an example of what I mean.

A female client wanted to know if a man she had met at a social function — whom she described as the greatest guy she'd ever met — was indeed Mr. Right. Her soul came out of her body during our session and told me to tell her, "Yes, this is the one." Her soul had an odd look on her face, so I knew there must have been something she wasn't sharing. Still, I related to the woman what her soul had said. About six months later, the woman came back for another reading. She told me that she had gotten into a relationship with the man, but that it had been the worst relationship she had ever been in.

They had since broken up, and she wanted to know why that one part of her last reading was so off.

I asked the woman's soul if she'd be willing to explain, and fortunately she did come out and talk to me. The soul said that she had some hard karma left over from a former lifetime with this particular guy, and she just had to go into the relationship again to pay back the karmic debt. The soul explained that if she had told her conscious mind that it was going to be a difficult relationship that would end badly, she would not have gone into it. I asked my client if this would have been true, and she said yes. The woman also said that when she was in the relationship she had a feeling that what she was going through with him was bigger than both of them and that it wasn't something she could simply walk away from.

Before we come into a new lifetime, a lot of planning goes on. Our soul will decide on goals it wants to achieve, and there are hundreds of life experiences it may choose to have in order to achieve those goals. For instance, there could be friends, spouses, and family members from past lives that we'll choose to be with either for the support they'll give us or to resolve some unfinished business. It's hard for us to accept the idea that our souls are in charge of our lives rather than ourselves, our minds/bodies, but it's true nevertheless.

If a person goes to a psychic to get a better understanding of why he or she is going through a difficult time, the psychic may only be given what information the person can handle hearing. The soul may choose not to give all the details if it will possibly prevent the person from going through an experience.

If our soul needs to have a certain experience, our guides and our intuition will encourage us to have it. Unfortunately, because society doesn't honor the soul and the bigger picture of our lives, we can end up feeling betrayed by our guides, our intuition, and God when we are led into a painful experience. If only we were taught to look at life through the eyes of our soul, then we would look for the gem in each life experience, however terrible it may seem in the moment, and welcome the benefits we receive from going through it.

ANOTHER TWIST ON GIVING THE WRONG INFORMATION

There's another explanation I've discovered about why people are sometimes given the wrong information, and it is that the universe has a way of *getting a person "off the fence"* in some area of life.

For instance, a young man once asked me if he should marry the young woman he was dating or move on. His guides told me to tell him that he was meant to marry her and that they would have several children. About three weeks after the reading, the young man called to say he was really upset with the information he'd received; after thinking it over, he realized he actually didn't want to marry her, and he wanted me to double-check with his guides to see if they may have made a mistake. His guides said that he had been on the fence about the direction of his life, and he needed to be pushed to make some decisions. He needed to really examine what his life would be like if he married this young woman — rather than continuing to tell himself that someday soon he would figure it out — and the information that he was "supposed" to marry her is exactly what he needed in order to do that and so move on with his life.

I've seen this kind of information come through for people who are stuck in miserable jobs, in bad relationships, or in financial troubles. It's a version of reverse psychology, where guides present advice that is the opposite of what is actually healthy or desired to force the person to "get off the fence," make the right decision, and move forward.

ONE MORE EXPLANATION: MISINTERPRETATION

Don't forget that the other explanation as to why the information in a psychic reading is off is simply because you misinterpreted the pictures you received or misunderstood the thoughts in your head. You may have interjected your own thoughts rather than actually hearing information from your guides, the guides of the person you're reading, or his or her soul. More than likely, in the first couple years of your development, this will be the reason that your friend or client says the reading wasn't accurate.

Whenever we misinterpret information, it's usually because we assume the meaning of an image too quickly. Sometimes we make assumptions based on the way the client asked the question, and sometimes we pick up the desires of the client. Sometimes the images seem so obvious we don't bother to question our guides or intuition any further. Here are some examples of how easy it is to misinterpret what we see.

- A client asked me in the springtime when I saw her father's health improving. The image that came was of an outdoor garden. I saw a big lawn, freshly mowed, with lots of people milling around a big table of food. Her dad seemed to be the focus of a lot of the conversations going on. I asked my guides when this was, and they showed me a calendar with a month beginning with *J*. I asked my intuition if this was June, and I got a *no*. I asked if it was July, and got *yes*. I assumed all of this meant he would be better by July, and that the image was of some sort of outdoor garden party to celebrate it. You can probably see what's coming, but I didn't. I told my client this, and she left very relieved. Then she called me in July to tell me she had just returned from her father's funeral. She said they had held the luncheon outside in a friend's yard! I felt awful, to say the least. This is a case where I asked the wrong question — I only asked *when* her father's health would improve, not *if* — and I didn't stop to verify whether my interpretation of the answer was correct.

- Here's another example, this one with a happier outcome: A client asked me if her husband was having an affair. I got an image of a man walking into an office, and I saw a blonde sitting at the receptionist desk. The blonde was very flirty, and I could feel a strong sexual energy between them. If I had stopped there, I would have assumed that the answer was *yes* — he was having an affair with a blonde in an office. Instead, because I knew it could be quite harmful if I got it wrong, I asked the picture to tell me more.

I saw the man go into his office and shut the door. Intuitively, this felt like the part of the message that was most important. I asked if they were having an affair and saw the word *no* in big letters. I asked if this was simple flirting, and I got a big *yes*. Then I saw another picture of the husband closing his office door.

I told the client exactly what I was seeing and feeling, and she smiled with a sense of relief. She said that her husband and the receptionist in his office had had an affair at one time, but that he now claimed that it was over between them. She was very happy to have that confirmed.

Sometimes I shudder to think of the damage we can do to people and their lives if we misinterpret the information. We have to be so careful all the time.

Remember, we are dealing with people's lives, and it's a tremendous responsibility. We are giving them information that could affect the rest of their lives. It's important to always remind the person you're reading to check with his or her own intuition as to whether the information you're giving is correct, and whether he or she should act on what you've said.

CHAPTER 4

BASIC PSYCHIC
DEVELOPMENT EXERCISES

*In this section I'll explain how to turn your abilities
on and off, and then I'll give you four simple exercises
that will help you develop and refine your psychic gifts.
Besides your desire to explore your psychic abilities, the
single most important thing you need at this point is
a partner or a group of like-minded people.*

GATHERING PEOPLE OF A LIKE MIND

One of the most important ingredients for your development is getting a group of people together who are
serious about psychic development. Ask friends and
co-workers (whom you trust and feel safe with) if any
of them would be interested in developing their abilities or helping you develop yours. If you have friends
who are interested in developing their psychic skills,
but they don't live near you, don't fret: you can practice together remotely. For example, you can do the

Names exercise (page 80) over the phone, via email, or through regular mail, and you could do the Photographs (page 91), Billets (page 97), and Psychometry (page 105) exercises via regular mail. Granted, it won't be the same as doing these in person, but if you don't have access to anyone who you can practice with in your area, then this option will work.

Once you've gathered a group of people interested in developing their psychic skills, I want you to make a commitment to meet every week, same time and same place, if possible, for continuity. It's helpful if you don't all know each other well already, because you're going to be doing readings on each other. If you have lots of prior knowledge about someone, you might not be sure whether the information you're receiving is real or based on what you already know about them, especially when you're first starting out.

Remember, it's crucial to choose people you feel safe with and who won't make fun of you. Our egos get in the way enough as it is when it comes to developing these gifts; don't make it harder on yourself by choosing practice partners whom you'll always feel you have to prove yourself to. That kind of situation can set up a huge block. None of us likes to be made fun of or put on the spot, so make sure you're not sabotaging your development by choosing unsupportive people to work with.

DOING THE EXERCISES TOGETHER

I'm going to teach you the same psychic development exercises my teacher taught me thirty-seven years ago. Some of these are going to work better for you than others, but I want you to do all of them several times until you find the ones that work best. Sometimes you might be blocked with one of the exercises, but what I've found is that this usually has more to do with the person you're practicing with than with the exercise itself. If you find you're stuck when doing one of these, try it with a different partner first rather than chucking the whole exercise.

If you have gathered a group of people, you need to split up into pairs to do the exercises. Then, every week, make sure you have a different partner, so that you don't read the same person every time. As soon as all of you are present each week, count off to determine which people will be paired up. This is easiest if the group is an even number. If there are six people in your group, for example, count off to three twice, and those people with matching numbers become partners for this week. Likewise, if you have eight people in the group, count to four twice; for ten people, count to five twice. If you have an odd number of people (such as five), create one group of three people, and have them read each other round-robin style, so that no one reads or is read twice.

Once you have your partner, you can do the exercises in one of two ways:

1. You can take turns with your partner, and as the information comes, you can say it out loud and get feedback as you go, or

2. You can both do the exercise at the same time, each of you writing down all of the information you're receiving on a piece of paper. Then, when you're both finished, you can review each other's paper and give feedback on accuracy.

In either case, whenever you are evaluating the psychic information of your partner, be sure you don't stretch the truth in order to make the information seem true. That's not going to help either of you develop your abilities. The information either fits or it doesn't!

Use these pages to brainstorm some people to partner with, or some ways to find like-minded people in your circle or community.

TURNING YOUR ABILITIES ON AND OFF

My guess is, if you're reading this book, you are aware of having some kind of psychic abilities, but they are hit or miss at this point. You can't call on them whenever you want to, and they might come when you least expect or want them to. This is very common with untrained psychic abilities, so don't get discouraged. It is possible to turn your abilities on and off at will.

Often my students tell me that once they've gotten their psychic channels opened up, they don't want to shut them down for fear that they'll never come back on. I can assure you, they will. In fact, in the beginning, it's just as important to be able to turn your abilities off so you don't develop a "third-eye headache."

When you're just starting out, you should do only a couple of exercises a week. Opening up your third eye and/or psychic ears takes time, and it's like exercising any muscle in your body: if you push yourself too hard, you'll hurt yourself. In this case, a third-eye headache feels like a tight band around your forehead, and aspirin isn't going to take it away. The only way to feel better is to shut down psychically and walk away from practicing for a while. The area in the middle of your forehead will always be sensitive, but in the beginning of your development, it will be especially so. Don't push it simply because you're excited. You have plenty of time to develop your abilities, so pace yourself.

I want you to do a simple exercise right now.

EXERCISE: OPEN YOUR THIRD EYE

Close your eyes and focus on the middle of your fore-head. Imagine there is a closed eye there, and next to it is a light switch, which is currently in the down, or off, position.

Now imagine turning the light switch on, and visual-ize your third eye slowly opening up (yes, it's really there). It may open just a tiny bit, or it may open up widely. It will open to some degree.

Now visualize a zipper on the top of your head. Imagine slowly unzipping it.

Now sit and focus on this picture (of an opened third eye and the energy above your head opened up) for about thirty seconds. What does your head feel like? It may be a subtle difference or a very obvious feeling. Just feel it.

Once you've done this, zip the zipper back up and turn off the light switch by your third eye. See your third eye close. Note what this feels like.

Now go through and do this entire exercise again. Turn on the light switch by your third eye, unzip the zip-per on top of your head, experience the sensation of being open psychically for about thirty seconds, and then close down your third eye and the energy on top of your head, noting how you now feel different.

This is all you need to do to psychically open yourself up and close down. You open up your third eye so that you can receive pictures, visions, or images, and by unzipping the zipper on top of your head, you open up your psychic ears so that you can receive messages.

It's important for you to know that you can control your gifts — that you can turn them on and turn them off when you want. It's also important for you to be able to recognize how it feels when they are on or off. This will help you discern between psychic messages and your own thoughts.

After I visualized opening up my third eye and psychic ears, I felt . . .

_____

_____

_____

_____

_____

_____

_____

_____

_____

_____

After I closed my third eye and zipped up the zipper, I felt . . .

_____

_____

_____

_____

_____

_____

_____

EXERCISE: OPEN TO UNIVERSAL TRUTH

Here is a more in-depth version of the opening exercise. Do this exercise before every practice session.

Sit in a chair, close your eyes, and take a few relaxing breaths. Ask your body to release stress and tension as you exhale. Notice any parts of your body that are feeling tight or in pain. When you inhale, visualize your breath going into that body part to bring calmness and ease the pain.

Let your body sink into the chair so that it feels completely supported.

Using your imagination, visualize roots coming out of the bottom of your feet, going down through the floor, and reaching at least six to ten feet into the ground. This will help your body feel grounded while you are opened up psychically.

Now visualize your third eye, located in the middle of your forehead, with the light switch next to it. Visualize turning the light switch to the on position and your third eye slowly opening. Next, visualize the zipper on the top of your head. Unzip the zipper, which in turn opens up your psychic ears.

You have now opened yourself up to Universal Truth. As you develop your abilities, you will become more and more aware of the feeling of this dimension, which is very light.

Next, go to your solar plexus and visualize a white light inside. This is where your intuition resides. Ask God (or, if you prefer, Universal Truth or Knowledge) to help you know the truth of the information you receive and to help you accurately interpret the information.

Now all systems are go, and you are ready to do some psychic work. Your third eye is open, you've opened your psychic ears, and you've got your wonderful helper, the inner voice (or intuition), ready to help you interpret the information you're about to receive.

ONE MORE THING: ASK QUESTIONS

Remember Columbo, that inquisitive TV detective played by Peter Falk, who was always driving people crazy with his countless questions? Well, sometimes when we're trying to get psychic information, we need to do the same thing. We need to put on our "Columbo coat" and ask the universe a lot of questions in order to get the information rolling in.

Here's a list of suggested questions I put together for my students so that instead of just waiting for information to come, they can go after it. You should do the same thing when doing the four exercises below; don't sit in absolute silence patiently waiting and waiting — ask questions! You can add your own questions to this list, but remember to always be respectful of people's boundaries. Don't ask questions that would breach anyone's privacy.

You can ask the universe questions like these:

- Is the person male or female?

- How tall is the person? Under five feet or over six feet?

- How old is the person? Under twenty or over thirty? Youthful, middle aged, or old?

- Does the person have a petite build, a medium build, or a heavy build?

- Does the person have light hair or dark hair? Blonde, brown, black, or red?

- What is the person's eye color? Brown, green, blue, or hazel?

- Does the person have any distinguishing features, such as eyeglasses, a beard or mustache, moles, freckles, or scars?

- Does the person have any health issues? (Notice your own body while tuning in. Do any parts hurt?)

- What is the person's marital status: married, single, divorced, or widowed? (Note: If the person is living with someone, it will come up as married.)

- Does the person have any children? How many and what sex?

- Is the person living or deceased? (Note: A deceased person's energy still feels alive, but it usually seems far away.)

- What is the person's profession?

- Does the person have any hobbies?

- Does the person play a musical instrument or have any artistic abilities?

- Does the person belong to an organized religion or follow a spiritual practice, or is he or she atheist?

There are also dozens of questions you can ask about a person's personality:

- Is the person gentle or aggressive?

- Is the person introverted or extroverted?

- Is the person pessimistic or optimistic?

- Is the person generally cautious or a risk taker?

- Is the person openly affectionate or reserved?

- Is the person moody or does he or she have an even temperament?

- Is the person serious or does he or she have a lively sense of humor?

- Is the person most often a leader or a follower?

- Is the person reliable and consistent or unreliable and inconsistent?

- Does the person guard his or her privacy or is the person open?

- Is the person more of an intellectual type or a creative type?

And finally, when you've run out of specific questions, don't forget to simply ask if there is any more information your guides can provide.

Now let's begin working with your partner to develop your psychic gifts.

EXERCISE: NAMES

In this exercise, you will practice tuning into a person's vibration by focusing on his or her first name. It's not necessary to have a full name. Have your partner give you the first name of someone he or she knows well. Write the name on a piece of paper, close your eyes, and ask the universe to give you clear, accurate information about this person. Remember to be respectful of personal boundaries, and ask for information that will help you know that you're on the right track.

Focus on the name. Say it over and over to yourself, either out loud or silently. When a thought or a picture comes into your mind, tell your partner or write it down (depending on how you're conducting the exercise) and then go back to the name. Continue repeating it to yourself. If a picture or thought of someone you know keeps coming into your mind, write down the characteristics that occur to you when you think of that person.

Be sure to tell your partner or write down the thoughts and images that seem goofy or insignificant —

you'll be surprised at how often the information that seems irrelevant is quite important. If you start "thinking" about what information you're getting, your intellect can actually block you, so just keep focusing on the name and write down whatever thoughts, pictures, or sensations come to you. Don't worry about being wrong. In the beginning, we just want to get things moving. The human tendency is to complicate matters, so remind yourself to keep it simple and focus on the name. If your head does get in the way and you start doubting what you're doing and thinking it's a waste of time, remind yourself that you're developing one of your gifts.

In the beginning, spend only about five minutes focusing on the name. When the time is up, or the information stops coming in, run each piece of information by your intuition for validation. It will let you know if the pictures, thoughts, or feelings are accurate.

For example, let's say that these are some of the things that came to you about the name *Sarah*:

- outgoing

- picture of a sports car

- mother

- blue dress

- pumpkins

- Johnny Mathis

Take one item at a time and focus on your intuition, asking it if the information is relevant. Each time, you will get an inner knowing of either *yes*, *no*, or *maybe*.

- Outgoing? *Yes.*

- A sports car? *Yes, but there's an odd feeling with it, like we don't have all the information.*

- Mother? *Yes.*

- Blue dress? *No.*

- Pumpkins? *Yes.*

- Johnny Mathis? *Yes.*

Now go back to the sports car and ask for clarity. Ask questions like:

- Does the person have a sports car? *No.*

- Does the person want a sports car? *Yes.*

After you've checked out all the information intuitively and feel satisfied with your answers, give your partner your list and get his or her feedback.

If none of the information is accurate, don't get discouraged. At first, the main goal is simply to get your psychic centers opened up and get the pictures and thoughts coming to you. We'll work a lot on accuracy later, so for now be patient and stay with it. The difficulty might have been with the name you were given, so ask your partner for another name and try again.

Let's talk through another example. Let's say this time your partner gives you the name *Tom*, but you happen to have a brother (or husband, cousin, or friend) with the same name, and you can't get past thinking about your relative. Ask your partner for the first initial of Tom's last name, but only the first initial. This is important for several reasons. One is that to tap into a person's energy, it's not necessary to know his or her last name. In addition, not providing a last name protects the person's anonymity. And last, sometimes names can throw us off. If we know the person's last name is, say, Goldstein, we might immediately assume the person is Jewish and start thinking of common Jewish characteristics or stereotypes. That's not being psychic — that's called playing it safe. Our mind (and ego) plays all kinds of tricks on us in order not to be wrong, but this gets in the way of hearing the truth about a person. That's why I always tell my students to stay away from people's last names and just stick with first names if possible and the first letter of the last name if necessary.

Now, getting back to Tom, let's say his last name begins with *T*. As before, focus all your attention on the name. When your mind starts to wander, come back to the name and repeat it over and over to yourself: *Tom T., Tom T., Tom T.* Soon, images (clairvoyance), thoughts (clairaudience), and feelings (clairsentience) will start to come. When they do, tell your partner or write them down:

- Airplanes

- Computers

- Gray suit

- Blueberries

- Wedding band

- Far away

Notice if your emotions change over the course of the exercise. While repeating Tom's name, do you find yourself feeling angry, sad, happy, melancholy, fearful? Write down any noticeable changes in your emotions or your physical body while focusing on his name. If you're a strong clairsentient, you may pick up through your body that the person has physical problems (if Tom has kidney problems, your lower back might suddenly start to hurt). When the images, thoughts, and feelings stop, run the list by your intuition for accuracy.

- Airplane? *Yes.*

- Computers? *Yes.*

- Gray suit? *Yes.*

- Blueberries? *Yes.*

- Wedding band? *No.*

- Far away? *Yes.*

Now let's take this a step further. Go down the list again, and for each item, ask your intuition for more clarification.

- Airplane: Does he own a plane? *No.* Does he fly airplanes? *No.* Does he travel a lot by airplane? *Yes.* Is there anything else significant about airplanes? *No.*

- Computer: Is he a computer programmer? *No.* Does he work with computers? *Yes.*

- Gray suit: Is there any significance to the gray suit other than that he wears one? *No.*

- Blueberries: Does he like blueberries? *Yes.* Is

there more significance here? *Yes*. Does he grow them? *Yes*. Is there more significance? *No*.

- Wedding band: No thoughts, feelings, or visions come when you say the words *wedding band*, so let it go and move on.

- Far away: Does he live far away? *Yes and no.* Hmm. Okay. Pin it down. Does he live in more than one place? *Yes*. Is one of them far away? *Yes*. Is there anything more significant than that? *No*.

When you feel satisfied with your answers, hand them to your partner for verification. Remember that you're in the beginning stages of understanding how all of this works, so look at every situation as a tool for learning. Pay as much attention to the possible sources of wrong information as you do to the information you get right. And again, be honest with your partner regarding accuracy. Real psychic information will not be fuzzy or "sort of" correct, so don't stretch to make the information fit if it really doesn't. Don't spare each other's feelings. That's not going to help you develop.

Before moving on to another exercise, ask the universe to clear you psychically. You may need to ask two or three times to make sure you are cleared of that person's energy. Whenever there is a lot of information and I can't seem to disconnect from a particular person, I imagine I have an eraser in my hand and visualize myself wiping off the area of my third eye. It works well.

Use these pages to record any thoughts, visions, feelings, fears, or blocks that come up for you while practicing the Names exercise.

EXERCISE: PHOTOGRAPHS

In this exercise, you will read photographs *without* looking at them. To begin, you and your partner should each get three to four photographs of people you know well, and one of them can be of you. Each photo should be of only one person, and preferably without any pets in the picture; pets have their own personalities, which can cause confusion when trying to read the picture. Put each photo in an envelope and mark the outside with the person's initials so that you will know whose picture you have given to your partner. Finally, exchange pictures one at a time with your partner, making sure the photo isn't visible through the envelope; if it is, hand over the envelope with the photograph facing down. For the first photo, you can tell your partner the person's sex, but that's all I want you to share.

Decide if you want to go one at a time, or both read the photos at the same time. If you choose to go one at a time, decide who is going to work first. If you decide to work at the same time, simply write down all your information and exchange these notes when you are both finished writing. If you are in a group of three, each one in the group should pass a photograph to the person on their right, and then everyone should read the photos at the same time. As in the Open to Universal Truth

exercise (page 75), begin by doing the opening-up visualizations: open your third eye, your psychic ears, and
your intuition.

To start, hold in your hand the envelope containing
the photo, and ask the universe, God, and your spirit
guides to give you clear, accurate information about this
person. Spend about five minutes on this. Write down
everything that comes to you, no matter how silly or
insignificant it seems (or, if you and your partner are taking turns, you can tell your partner out loud what you're
getting). When it feels like there's no more information
coming, run the list by your intuition for accuracy. Don't
get frustrated in the beginning if this seems tedious or
time-consuming; it will become second nature after a
while. When you've finished checking with your intuition, you and your partner should exchange lists and
then give each other honest feedback about your
accuracy.

Only after you've finished the reading and gotten
feedback should you both look at the pictures. You might
be surprised at how the person in the photo looks
because it may be very different from what you saw in
your third eye. If this happens, don't be alarmed. Our
minds are always working, and your mind may have put
together a composite sketch based on random information you were picking up. Return to the list of attributes
you wrote down and discuss them with your partner.

Work with each other. Share any information about the person in the photo that would help each of you understand the images, thoughts, and feelings you got.

When you've finished discussing your readings on the first photograph, ask the universe to clear you of the person's energy. Then do the next picture, except this time I want you to give your partner the first name of the person in the photograph. I want you to see the difference it makes when you also have the person's name.

You may find that you were very accurate with the first picture but not so accurate with the second one, and this could be for a couple of reasons:

1. The person in the second picture isn't as easy to read.

2. Your ego got in the way, wanting to make sure you were right again the second time.

If you don't get any given reading right, don't be too hard on yourself. This is all very normal. You will go through various stages of being nervous, wanting to be right, feeling afraid when you are right, and worrying about being wrong. We go through a lot of changes as we develop our abilities, which is another reason why I want you to keep a journal. Write out all your thoughts and feelings about your psychic abilities — your frustrations, excitement, anxiety, fears, and goals. Also, if you're aware of any blocks, write those down, too. This is definitely a journey, and it's going to take some time to "get there." Try to enjoy every step along the way.

Use these pages to record any thoughts, visions, feelings, fears, or blocks that come up for you while practicing the Photographs exercise.

EXERCISE: BILLETS

Longtime late-night talk-show host Johnny Carson played a character named "Carnac the Magnificent." Carnac was a turbaned fortune-teller who would hold up to his third eye a piece of paper with a hidden question written on it and tell viewers the answer. Those pieces of paper with questions on them are called *billets*.

Back in the 1960s and '70s, there were billet readers who would hold sessions for the public to come and get psychic advice. These gatherings were usually held in a large convention room or church. I attended several, and they went like this: You'd go in, pay your five dollars, and get a piece of paper to write a question on. You were supposed to address the billet to one of your deceased relatives or spirit guides, ask them a question about your life, and sign it in a loving way. You were to hold the billet for about thirty seconds while thinking about your question, then you would fold it twice to make sure the billet reader couldn't possibly read your question, and someone would come along with a basket (like the collection plate at church) to gather them all and take them to the reader standing at the podium. An assistant would put cotton balls on the reader's eyes, followed by a blindfold. Then for the next couple of hours, the reader would reach into the basket and take out a billet, hold it up to his or her third eye, and proceed to give the answer out loud.

To help the crowd distinguish whose question it was, the reader would always say something like, "This question is for someone on the right side of the room whose first name starts with an *F*. You wrote this to your sister in spirit, and she says to tell you that the answer to your question is that you have to be patient until springtime and then you will get the guidance you are praying for." The reader was often more specific in his or her answers, but you never knew what to expect. Sometimes the reader would say something like, "This billet was written by a person on the left side of the room who was going to wear a red sweater today, but changed her mind at the last minute." And then the reader would proceed to give the answer.

Never once did the reader look at a question, but the skeptics all said billet readers had hidden microphones and tiny mirrors inside the blindfolds, and that's how they knew who was in the crowd. (Oh, brother!)

Now, it's your turn. I want you to do billets with your partner. Both of you take a piece of paper and write a question to one of your guides or a deceased relative. The question can be anything that you would like advice about. Then, thank the person for helping you and sign the billet, just as if you had written a letter. For example:

Dear Grandma,

I'm thinking about applying for a teaching job. Do you think this is a wise move, and can you tell me a good time to do this? Thank you.

Love, Jake

Fold the piece of paper twice and hold it in your hands for about thirty seconds while you focus on your question. After you've both done this, exchange billets.

Before trying to psychically read the billets, make sure you both do the Open to Universal Truth exercise (page 75). Then, without looking at the billets, close your eyes and either hold the billet up to your third eye, as Johnny Carson did, or hold the billet in your hands and simply focus your attention on it. Ask God or your guides to help you receive clear, accurate information that will help answer your partner's question. As images, thoughts, and feelings start coming, write them down, either on the outside of the billet or on a separate piece of paper. Every time the information stops coming, ask if there's more information for this question.

Students sometimes groan about billets, but that's just their ego talking. They feel like they don't have any control over the outcome of the reading since they don't know what the question is. Actually, *not* knowing the question is what makes this such a good exercise, since it trains you to be an open channel for information.

Write down everything that comes to you. Don't assume anything is stupid or insignificant. Remember, the only way to learn is to pay attention to everything. It's trial and error at first. Whether you get it right or get it wrong, always learn from it!

Remember, too, to work with your partner. Don't play *stump the psychic* by trying to trick your partner with fake or insignificant questions. You're in this together. Ask authentic questions in the billets and give honest feedback about the answers. When you're finished with one billet, be sure to clear yourself before doing another one.

If the answer your partner gives you in response to your question just doesn't seem to fit, one of two things might be going on.

1.   If there were two questions you were think-
     ing of writing, the answer you got may apply
     to the other question you were going to ask.

2.   It could simply mean your partner didn't get
     accurate information.

When starting out with these exercises, I suggest only doing a couple per session. You can work up to doing more, but remember, this is a process, and you don't want a third-eye headache. When you've decided you're done doing billets for the day, do the Close Up When You Finish exercise described at the end of this chapter (page 111).

Use these pages to record any thoughts, visions, feelings, fears, or blocks that come up for you while practicing the Billets exercise.

EXERCISE: PSYCHOMETRY

A lot of psychics do *psychometry*. This is holding and reading a personal object, such as a piece of jewelry, an article of clothing, or a favorite toy. Everything we have and use — our clothing and furniture, our offices and bedrooms, our cars and toys, and especially our jewelry — has our vibes in it. (Metal objects are preferred by psychics doing readings because metal holds people's energy or vibes longer than other materials.)

For this next exercise, I want you to bring a few pieces of jewelry for your partner to read. One piece can be yours, but the others need to belong to a friend or relative you know well. Avoid antique and second-hand jewelry if at all possible; these can be difficult to read because they have more than one person's vibes in them, which will make it difficult to verify the information that you receive.

(Incidentally, if you are someone who loves antique jewelry, I would suggest smudging it with sage after you purchase it. To do this, burn some sage and hold the object in the smoke for a few minutes, asking the universe to clear it of all the vibes it's holding. This is especially important for psychic people because we're ultrasensitive to begin with, and wearing someone else's vibes all day can actually drain our energy. I also suggest saging new pieces of jewelry after you buy them — a lot of people may have handled those pieces before you.)

Before starting the exercise, open up psychically using the Open to Universal Truth exercise (page 75). When you've finished the opening exercise, exchange a single piece of jewelry with your partner. Hold the jewelry in your hands and close your eyes. Ask the piece of jewelry to tell you what information it's holding about the person who wears it. As the information starts to come, write it down on a piece of paper. Remember not to censor the information no matter how stupid or insignificant it may seem. Just let it flow to you. If your ego gets in the way and you start worrying about being wrong, remind yourself that it's okay to make mistakes and that this is how you learn to discern between significant and insignificant information.

When you feel done receiving information, run everything by your intuition for validation, and then share the information with your partner. Be sure to give each other honest feedback. Remember to clear yourself before moving on to another piece of jewelry. When you are finished with the Psychometry exercises, be sure to shut down psychically using the Close Up When You Finish exercise (page 111).

Use these pages to record any thoughts, visions, feelings, fears, or blocks that come up for you while practicing the Psychometry exercise.

EXERCISE: CLOSE UP WHEN YOU FINISH

When you're finished doing your practice exercises, you need to not only clear yourself of the people you've been reading, but to shut yourself down psychically. Do the following after every session. This meditation is a combination of the closing visualizations described earlier under "Turning Your Abilities On and Off" (page 72) and the Clearing exercise in chapter 2 (page 33).

Close your physical eyes, take a couple of deep relaxing breaths, and release any tension that might be sitting in your body. Visualize the light switch by your third eye, which is on right now. Imagine switching it off, and your third eye closing. Then visualize zipping up the top of your head.

Now ask the universe or God to clear you:

Please clear my body.
Clear my body.
Please clear my mind.
Clear my mind.
Please clear my soul.
Clear my soul.
Please clear me psychically.
Clear me psychically.

Last, I want you to cough. This will clear your throat center in case you held back some words during the reading.

Take a couple of relaxing breaths and open your eyes when you feel refreshed. Now you're back in this reality and can go about your everyday business.

It's very important to do this clearing exercise, because you don't want to carry any of the people you've just read around with you. If after doing it you still feel somewhat spacey, again ask the universe to clear you, and then ground yourself further by doing one or several of the suggestions listed in chapter 2 under "Stay Grounded" (page 25).

MEDITATION

On the days when you're not practicing these four exercises, I want you to spend a minimum of five minutes sitting in silence, meditating, and focusing on the white light deep inside in the area of your solar plexus. This is a good discipline for anyone to learn. While you're focusing on the light, feel the calmness and safety of this light and the wisdom within it. If your mind wanders, keep coming back to the light.

When sitting in silence, you can ask your guides to make themselves known to you. Ask if they have any direction or guidance for you regarding your life. Ask

God to reveal Him- or Herself to you. If your mind starts to wander, refocus on the white light.

As you get more comfortable meditating, extend the time. The longer you spend in silent communication with your inner voice (God) and your guides, the stronger the connection will become. As you continue to grow spiritually, you'll want to spend more time meditating on the light, and I encourage you to do so. This is one of the best ways for us to establish conscious contact with God.

If you find you have a difficult time sitting and concentrating in silence, that doesn't mean meditation isn't for you. Almost everyone struggles with this at first. If you prefer having some background noise, go ahead and create whatever environment makes you most comfortable. Don't hassle yourself about it. My brother Michael usually has some kind of background noise, like a stereo or TV playing low, when he meditates or does psychic readings because he says distractions help him hear spirits more easily. Experiment and see what way works best for you.

LET YOUR LIGHT SHINE

Developing your abilities is a natural process. It is a journey along which you will gain much wisdom. Don't try to hurry it or take shortcuts. Consider whatever you're going through right now as exactly what you should be going through, and when you're ready for the next stage of development, it will arrive. Trust me.

Do you know the difference between a fortune-teller and a prophet, *besides* psychic development and lots of practice? It's knowing that we're worthy of developing ourselves to our highest potential. It's discovering the power within ourselves and letting our light shine.

I wish you the very best on your journey, and don't forget to practice, practice, practice!

CHAPTER 5

PROGRESS JOURNAL

*As you progress in your psychic development,
use these pages to record your thoughts, feelings,
fears, blocks, anticipations, expectations, and
visions. And remember, try to write something
every day. Later, you'll enjoy looking back
and seeing how much you've grown.*

ECHO BODINE is a renowned psychic, spiritual teacher, and healer. She has appeared on many national television programs, including NBC's *Later Today, Sally Jesse Raphael, Sightings*, and *The Other Side*. She is the author of several books about psychic and spiritual phenomena, including *Echoes of the Soul; Hands That Heal; A Still, Small Voice; Relax, It's Only a Ghost;* and *Dear Echo*.

Echo lectures widely on life after death, living by intuition, and developing psychic abilities. She can be reached at echo@echobodine.com, or:

P. O. Box 385321
Bloomington, MN 55438

Visit Echo's website for information about her books, videos, and audios: www.echobodine.com